THE GREAT BOOK OF ANIMAL KNOWLEDGE

RHINOS

Horned Beasts of the African Grasslands

Introduction

Photo by bobrayner (flickr.com/ bobrayner) via: freeforcommercialuse.org

Rhinoceros, or rhinos, are amazing and massive animals. There are five different types of rhinos, ranging from the white rhino, the biggest rhino; to the Sumatran rhino, the smallest. The name rhinoceros means "horn nose" referring to their horns above their noses. They are the second largest land mammals in the world after the elephant.

What Rhinos Look Like

Photo by QUOI Media Group (flickr.com/quoimedia) via: freeforcommercialuse.org

Rhinos can have one or two horns right on top of its head above its nose. They have big, long faces with small eyes. Rhinos have thick, protective skin, folding at some parts in their body. They are usually gray in color, but sometimes they have different colors, depending on the kind of rhino.

Size and Weight

Photo by 5of7 (flickr.com/53936799@N05) via: freeforcommercialuse.org

Rhinos are huge animals. The largest rhinos weigh about 6,000 pounds! That's about as heavy as two cars! The smallest rhinos only weigh 1,300 pounds. The rhino's normal height is about 5 to 6 feet.

Senses

Photo by Ryan Poplin (flickr.com/ poplinre) via: freeforcommercialuse.org

Did you know that a rhino will hardly notice you if you stand very still a few feet away from it? That's because a rhino's eyesight is very poor. To make up for the poor eyesight though, rhinos have a very strong sense of hearing and smell. Their sense of touch isn't very good either, but the soles of their feet are sensitive.

Horns

Photo by Ruth Hartnup (flickr.com/ ruthanddave) via: freeforcommercialuse.org

The most unique part of a rhino is its horn. The rhino's horn is not made of bone but it's made of keratin, the same mineral found in your fingernails! Some rhinos have two horns while others just have one. Rhinos use their horns for posturing (using posture to protect their territory from other leading male rhinos), for defending themselves when they get into fights, and digging for food and water when food and water aren't abundant. Their horns are also used for other things like testing the mud if it's not too thick to enter.

Where Rhinos Live

Photo by Anup Shah (flickr.com/anupshah) via: freeforcommercialuse.org

Rhinos are found in parts of Africa and Asia. They mostly stay in grasslands or savannas. They also stay in places where mud is readily available, because mud keeps rhinos cool and also kills ticks in their skins.

What Rhinos Eat

Photo by oatsy40 (flickr.com/ oatsy40) via: freeforcommercialuse.org

Rhinos are herbivorous, meaning they eat only plants. They do not hunt other animals. Rhinos are not picky with their food. They can eat almost any kind of fruit, stems, twigs, grasses, and leaves. Rhinos can last several days without water and still be able to survive because of the moisture from the plants they eat.

What Rhinos Do

Photo by Sam Felder (flickr.com/ samfelder) via: freeforcommercialuse.org

Rhinos spend most of their mornings and nights eating. But at the hottest time of the day (the afternoon) the rhinos either sleep or take a bath in the mud.

Baby Rhinos

Photo by Kool Cats Photography over 3 MillionViews (flickr.com/ katsrcool) via: freeforcommercialuse.org

Female rhinos can only give birth to one baby rhino (called a calf) at a time. Calves can start eating grass and plants when they're just 1 week old, but still drink milk from their mother. The young rhino has no horn at birth, so they depend entirely on their mother for protection. They can take care of themselves when they reach the age of 3 years.

The Life of a Rhino

Photo by Jeppestown (flickr.com/ jeppestown) via: freeforcommercialuse.org

Though rhinos often live alone, they sometimes form groups, called crashes. These groups are usually made up of a female and her offspring.

A strong male rhino rules over an area of land, and will allow weaker male rhinos to live in his territory. Female rhinos are free to go around different territories.

Life Span

Photo byJon O (flickr.com/jon360) via: freeforcommercialuse.org

Rhinos can live for 40 or 50 years! But most of them don't reach that age because of the serious threats of poachers, people who kill them for their horns.

Mating

Photo by Mike (flickr.com/ downeym) via: freeforcommercialuse.org

Because rhinos like being alone, they only see each other when it's mating season. Male and female rhinos usually fight a lot while mating, sometimes giving each other serious wounds. After mating, the pair goes their separate ways, and may never see each other again!

Communicating

Rhinos can communicate with each other in many different ways. They can communicate through scent (usually the spraying of urine to mark a territory as theirs), vocals (snorts, growls, squeals, moos, and even a trumpet sound), or through body language.

Predators

Photo by Valentina Storti (flickr.com/ fwooper7) via: freeforcommercialuse.org

Because rhinos are large and powerful, they are not really threatened by other animal predators. Baby rhinos, though, are still in danger of predators, such as crocodiles or lions, because they don't have the size or strength to protect themselves.

Poachers

Photo by Jean (flickr.com/ 7326810@N08) via: freeforcommercialuse.org

The biggest danger to rhinos are poachers, the people who kill the rhinos to get their horns. About a hundred rhinos are killed each year by poachers. Because of this, rhinos are now endangered, which means there are very few left.

Bird Friends

Photo by Harvey Barrison (flickr.com/ hbarrison) via: freeforcommercialuse.org

Did you know that a rhino's best friend is a bird called the oxpecker? It's true! The bird eats the ticks and other bugs on the rhino's skin. They also warn a rhino ahead of time that danger is coming by making a lot of noise. Rhinos allow these birds to stay on top of them and provide food for them (the ticks and bugs).

Black Rhinos

Photo by Alastair Rae (flickr.com/ merula) via: freeforcommercialuse.org

The black rhino isn't really black, but gray! They were named black rhinos because the mud they roll in make them look almost black. Black rhinos are found in Africa. Their mouth shape is different from their African relative, the white rhino. Black rhinos have a pointed upper lip which helps them get fruits and leaves from branches.

White Rhinos

Photo by Son of Groucho (flickr.com/sonofgroucho) via: freeforcommercialuse.org

Just like the black rhino, white rhinos are also gray (but they can also be brown) and they're also found in Africa. The white rhino is the largest of the five kinds of rhinos. They have square lips for grazing grass. They're more social than the black rhinos, but still prefer being alone.

Sumatran Rhino

Photo by W. Alan Baker (flickr.com/ walanbaker) via: freeforcommercialuse.org

The Sumatran rhino is the smallest of the rhino family. It is the only kind of rhino that is covered with patches of stiff hair. Unlike most of the other rhinos, the Sumatran rhinos are colored dark red-brown. Their horns are no more than a hump. They are found in parts of Asia.

Javan Rhinos

Photo by Oliver Beckstein (flickr.com/ orbeckst) via: freeforcommercialuse.org

Javan rhinos, also called the lesser one-horned rhino or Sunda rhino, have only one horn. Their skin has a number of loose folds. There are only about 50 Javan rhinos left, making them the fewest kind of rhino. They are found in Indonesia, Vietnam, and other places nearby.

Indian Rhinos

Photo by Narasimman Jayaraman (flickr.com/narasclicks) via: freeforcommercialuse.org

The Indian rhinos also have only one horn. Their segmented body makes it look like they have a natural body armor. Despite their size, they are very quick and can easily change directions while running. Indian rhinos are found mainly in Northern India and Nepal.

Get the next book in this series!

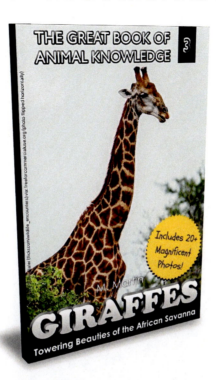

GIRAFFES: Towering Beauties of the African Savanna

Log on to Facebook.com/GazelleCB for more info

Tip: Use the keyphrase "The Great Book of Animal Knowledge" when searching for books in this series.

For more information about our books, discounts and updates, please Like us on Facebook!

Facebook.com/GazelleCB

73062444R00015

Made in the USA
San Bernardino, CA
31 March 2018